This book is dedicated to all who find Nature not an adversary to conquer and destroy, but a storehouse of infinite knowledge and experience linking man to all things past and present. They know conserving the natural environment is essential to our future well-being.

SHENANDOAH
THE STORY BEHIND THE SCENERY®

Shenandoah National Park, *located in northwestern Virginia, established in 1935, preserves an outstanding portion of the Blue Ridge Mountains, historic Shenandoah Valley and the Piedmont.*

by Hugh Crandall

Hugh Crandall, free-lance writer and photographer, has contributed a considerable portion of his efforts to the National Park Service since his retirement from the U.S. Navy in 1960. He lived and worked for many years in Shenandoah National Park, and knows the many moods of Shenandoah, of which he writes so intimately. Hugh is the author of two other books in this series: *Yellowstone* and *Grand Teton.*

Front cover: October colors in Shenandoah Valley, photo by Tom Till Inside front cover: Trilliums in late spring, photo by Williard Clay. Title page: Tufted titmouse, photo by Aggie Crandall. Page 2/3: Autumn foliage along Skyline Drive, photo by Jeff Gnass.

Edited by Mary L. Van Camp. Book design by K. C. DenDooven.
Fourth Printing • Revised Edition, 1990
SHENANDOAH: THE STORY BEHIND THE SCENERY © 1990 KC PUBLICATIONS, INC.
LC 88-82821. ISBN 0-88714-027-0.

Shenandoah National Park is mountain forest—thousands of acres of mountain forest. Over every one of those acres people have walked, and over each of them people will walk again. Yet most of Shenandoah's mountain acres are wilderness. They are wild in the sense that streams are allowed to flow and rocks to crumble and living things are allowed to live, free of human intervention. The plants and animals of Shenandoah are there, not because they are nurtured by people, but because they are nurtured by elements of the Blue Ridge Mountain habitat. The plants and animals that are *not* there are absent, not because people have weeded them out, but because their genetic natures make them better suited to different environments.

Shenandoah has not always been even so gently wild as it is today. Before the establishment of the park in the 1930s, and before Park Service principles of conservation were applied in the area, the northern Blue Ridge had been heavily used. From place to place the extent of use varied from hunting and gathering to stock grazing, mining, timbering, and total clearing.

Any land left undisturbed will slowly reestablish the vegetation most suited to it, and each

A sense of the past permeates the hemlock and yellow birch groves near Hoover Camp

vegetative type will attract the animal life most suited to *it*. Thus Shenandoah National Park, now relatively undisturbed throughout 95 percent of its area, and despite increasing hindrance from poor air quality, ozone concentrations, and acid rain, has largely reverted to a forest ecosystem.

That restoration has caused Shenandoah to be called a "recycled park." Although it was established in response to a need for a national park close to the population centers of the East Coast, today it serves another purpose as well. It demonstrates the capability of the natural world to restore and to the normal condition that is dictated by its soil, topography, and climate.

The rocks that form the spine of the Blue Ridge, the angle of the sun at Shenandoah's latitude, the temperature ranged throughout its elevations, and the precipitation pattern of the air masses that move across the park—these factors once generated, and are now regenerating, the hardwood forest communities natural to northern Virginia mountains. The story of Shenandoah tells of the way these natural forces have affected the land. It also chronicles the continuing change in the American philosophy of land use.

5

The Ancient Mountains

The story of the rocks of Shenandoah comes first because it is the weathering of the rocks which forms the soil, which in turn supports the forest, which feeds and shelters the animals. It is a history of alternate upliftings and downwarpings of this part of the earth's surface. It is a play in very slow motion, enacted over an enormous period of what people call "real time." It is still going on.

The oldest character in this play is a group of granitic rocks, some of which make up Old Rag Mountain. Geologic time covers periods too vast to be subjectively meaningful to most people, including perhaps geologists themselves. A million years is not easily comprehended by minds with a life span of less than a hundred. But "years" are our largest handy units of time, so we have to use them—*one billion* of them—to measure the age of the "ragged" rocks of Old Rag Mountain. That's ten million centuries, or a million millennia, or five-hundred-thousand times the span of the Christian era—still incomprehensible!

Because granitic rocks are formed only at very great depths in the earth's crust, they often constitute the deepest known strata, and are thus called "basement" rocks. Some time after the formation of the basement rocks we now know as Old Rag granite, a slow uplift of this part of the earth's crust began and continued for many millions of years. During that time the miles of other rocks lying above the granite were gradually eroded, and what had been the deepest strata became exposed at the surface. Then streams, and perhaps glaciers, carved thousand-foot-deep valleys into the granite itself.

The surface at that time was bare of vegetation, except perhaps for a few patches of primitive algae. Trees, ferns, and mosses had not yet evolved and there were no animals. The naked rock baked in the sun, then chilled and cracked in the rain. Small particles of rock were blown by the wind to knock more particles loose and expose a new surface to the next period of baking by the sun. The valleys accumulated gravel, sand, and fragments of weathered granite. Granite ledges collected boulders and thin pockets of sand beneath granite cliffs. The hills became rounded. Three hundred million years had passed since those

Some 700 million years ago the rock that forms the crest of Stony Man Mountain was molten basalt pouring out of fissures in the earth's crust. It was later buried for 300 million years under thousands of feet of ocean sediment before being lifted again to the surface and folded into mountains.

JEFF GREENBERG

rounded hills were basement rock far below the surface!

As the crust continued its slow uplift, cracks developed, often extending for miles across the surface and penetrating completely through the crust to the upper mantle layer, perhaps 30 miles beneath. Then, 700- or 800-million years ago, volcanic activity began and continued for a considerable period of time. Recurring at intervals of many years—even hundreds of years—molten lava of the mantle layer was forced upward through the fissures and flowed over the barren land. The first eruptions covered the gravel floors of the valleys; successive outpourings eventually filled the valleys and covered even the highest peaks.

In the Big Meadows-Stony Man area there is evidence of 12 distinct flows, which collectively produced a depth of 1,800 feet of basalt. There may have been many more such flows, but if so, they have been worn away by millions of years of erosion.

The total deposition of lava from these flows—the Catoctin Formation—has undergone metamorphism, altering its mineral structure from the original basalt to greenstone, a dense, gray-green rock. The greenstone retains the fineness of grain of the parent rock, which cooled too quickly for the formation of large crystals. It demonstrates one other characteristic of surface-cooled lavas: As each molten mass cooled and solidified, it contracted, and the surface cracked into innumerable four- to eight-sided figures, the way a patch of mud cracks as it dries and shrinks. Continued cooling caused the cracks to penetrate deeper and deeper, eventually forming large columns of rock.

The tunnel that leads the Skyline Drive through Mary's Rock is cut from granodiorite of about the same age as Old Rag granite. But it also cuts through a dike of greenstone formed from one of the fissures that led basaltic lava to the surface.

This columnar jointing can be seen at several places in the park, including Franklin Cliffs, Crescent Rock, and Little Devils Stairs. A small pile of these columns is exposed along the Whiteoak Canyon Trail in the Limberlost.

As each flow of lava stopped, the fissure through which it had reached the surface remained plugged with cooling basalt. These plugs, too, were altered by metamorphism. Such a greenstone dike can be seen at the north end of Marys Rock tunnel. A stretch of the Ridge Trail to the summit of Old Rag runs along a dike. Although greenstone is a very hard rock, it erodes faster than granite; thus the corridor through which the trail passes has high granite walls and a greenstone floor.

When the entire period of lava outpourings came to an end, the former surface of rolling granite hills and stream valleys lay buried beneath a layer of basalt many hundreds of feet thick. The new surface was a level, featureless plain. It in turn began to be acted upon by the inexorable processes of erosion.

The surface rock of most of the central section of Shenandoah is greenstone, the metamorphosed remains of old lava flows. Outcroppings such as these on Bearfence Mountain have typically weathered to shades of gray. Only recent fractures display the green color that gives the rock its name.

Blooming mountain laurel softens the harshness of naked rock at Franklin Cliffs, and the typical Blue Ridge haze softens the outlines of the Appalachian Mountains across the valley.

Then the massive forces that had lifted the basement rocks thousands of feet, while erosion stripped them of their cover until they were exposed at the surface, came slowly to a halt and reversed themselves. It is probable that North America, South America, Europe, and Africa were once joined in one huge continent. About 600 million years ago, that "mother continent" began to pull apart, and gradually the Americas separated from Europe and Africa. As the split widened, shallow seas spread across much of what is now eastern North America, western Europe, and northwestern Africa. Those seas covered much of the present area of the Appalachian Mountains, including the Blue Ridge, for most of the subsequent 350 million years.

During that immense period of time, the Catoctin lavas that had buried the basement granitics were themselves buried under water-laid sediment which eventually compacted into 30,000 feet of sedimentary rock. Layers of mud compacted into shale. Layers of sand became first sandstone and then quartzite. Mats of algae and the shells of countless generations of sea animals formed bands of limestone.

Exposed rocks in the southern section of the park are what remains of the sedimentary deposits that were left by the sea that covered this area for over 300 million years. Over that vast time, and under great pressure from overlying layers, deposits of sand became sandstone and then the quartzite shown here in the walls of the Big Run drainage system.

HUGH CRANDALL

FORMING THE APPALACHIANS

The time was 300 million years ago; the formation of the Appalachian Mountains began!

It is helpful at this point to digress from the strict chronology of the narrative of the rocks of Shenandoah. For the entire period of this story, as well as for the several billion years before the story began, the planet Earth has been reacting to the various forces applied to it. It has been getting colder (or warmer), contracting (or expanding), slowing down (or speeding up). Because these processes have occurred so very slowly, within a time scale so much more immense than the few millennia in which mankind has played a part, it is difficult to backtrack far enough to be certain of exactly what has been happening.

In the meantime, the earth proceeds on its own majestic way, indifferent to the ways of those who occupy it. So far, at least, for all mankind's effect on the thin layer in which we live, our species has had no appreciable effect on the planet as a whole. Meanwhile, even the slightest of the

Not all the original sedimentary rocks formed under that ancient sea were metamorphosed. Here, forming a narrow gap through which Big Run passes, is shale, a sedimentary rock that is the compressed and bonded deposits of ultra-fine, clayey material.

earth's shiftings and adjustments has a considerable effect on people, and we have tried to understand and explain these phenomena.

One of the puzzles we have tried to understand is the behavior of the earth that results in mountains. At first we explained it through myths and legends, some charming, but none intellectually satisfying. Later, scientific theories were not much better, partly because the observational base has been too short.

To illustrate: A snapshot (one-sixtieth of a second) of an elderly man reveals, through the deep vertical creases between his eyebrows, that during his life he frequently frowned. At that point the theories begin: (1) he is an irascible man who has spent a great deal of his life in anger; (2) he is a slow-witted man, baffled by the complexities of life; (3) he is a near-sighted man who compensates for his physical defect by squinting. All three theories are plausible, but none can be accepted as certain. To change one of them from "plausible" to "probable," a longer observational base than that one-sixtieth of a second is needed.

So it is with the Appalachian Mountains, the "wrinkles" in the earth's crust which extend northeasterly from Alabama to Newfoundland. Our time of observation has been like that snapshot. It has been too short to enable us to say more than that a tremendous force from the southeast crumpled the formerly flat layers of rocks into folds. And the *nature* of that force has been a mystery.

In recent times imaginative thinking and advanced instruments have accomplished what had seemed impossible; they have extended the observational base far into the past, to a time long before there were people to observe directly.

The ages of rocks can now be determined with considerable accuracy by radioactive analysis. Magnetic analysis can provide information as to the original orientation of rock strata and, from that, data as to the amount and direction of whatever shifting has occurred. More precise measuring of seismic waves yields more reliable clues concerning the nature of the earth at depths too great for direct observation. New instruments provide a basis for greater knowledge of the ocean depth and the shape and nature of the ocean floor. Computers speed integration and analysis of the informational bits. In the light of new data, the old, nearly discarded theory of *continental drift* has taken on new meaning.

The combining of the contributions of geologists, geophysicists, and oceanographers has resulted in a new geologic concept of the earth,

WILLARD CLAY

This lichen-covered greenstone is a soil factory at work. Sun and wind and rain and the acid secretions of lichens gradually wear away even the hardest of rocks and release their minerals to be available to higher plants. The leafy green of Allegheny stonecrop precariously rooted in small soil pockets testifies to the effectiveness of the inevitable process of erosion. Water, freezing in the cracks, and the pressure of growing roots will split off large boulders to become annexes of this factory somewhere farther down the mountain.

one which has wide acceptance and is moving steadily toward the "probable." In this new *plate tectonics* theory (reduced to simple form), the earth's rocky crust is divided into huge plates which rest on a fluid mantle layer, in the manner of ice floes, loosely frozen together, floating on an arctic sea.

The mantle is in motion, possibly as a result of convection currents caused by radioactive heating. The motion is very slow (the highest lateral velocity has been estimated at only five inches a year)—but the force is incredible! As the upper surface of the mantle moves, the plates shift—sometimes drifting apart, sometimes coming together. When adjoining plates are pressed together, the force may be great enough to fold them into mountains.

So those of us who were not really comfortable with "mysterious" forces can now choose instead a force that is merely "incomprehensible," and we can continue with the chronology of the story of the Blue Ridge Mountains.

About 300 million years ago a slow, massive motion within the mantle of the earth caused two huge crustal plates to press together with tremendous force—a force that was sustained for a great many centuries and eventually buckled one of the plates along its edge to form the Appalachian Range. Perhaps, to most of us, this explanation is no more comprehensible than the older "unknown force from the southeast," but to an increasing number of scientists it is much more satisfying.

The maximum height of the ancestral Appalachians is not known. We do know that about 30,000 feet of sedimentary rock and many additional feet of greenstone have been worn away from above 4,000-foot-high Hawksbill and Stony Man mountains. If the rate of uplift always matched the rate of erosion, they obviously could never have been any higher than they are today. But, if at some time during the hundred million years of their formation, the rate of uplift was faster, then they surely would have at some point been much higher than they are today—perhaps as high as the Rocky Mountains are now. Whatever their maximum height, they are believed to have reached it nearly 200 million years ago.

Since that time, the principal geologic activity has been erosion—inevitable and inexorable. During the mountain-building era, sections of the original horizontal layers of rock had been tilted to nearly vertical by the folding of the crust. The layers of harder rock eroded slowly, and now stand as ridges; softer layers (the limestones and sandstones) eroded faster to form valleys; the valleys served as conduits to carry off the products of the wearing away of the ridges.

In some places the Shenandoah River is still cutting through underlying rock, but in other places it meanders through thick layers of sediment. The Potomac River to the north of the park and the James River to the south are older than the mountains themselves; they maintained their ancestral courses by carving gaps through the ridges as the mountains were uplifted.

On the summit of cloud-shrouded Hawksbill Mountain the uneven lengths of the branches of the weather-stunted firs reveal the direction of the prevailing wind.

WILLIAM A. BAKE

The stony crest of the Blue Ridge Mountains typically forms the foreground of panoramic scenes of the lowland farms on either side. Here the Allegheny Mountains to the west are faintly visible across the Shenandoah Valley.

CARR CLIFTON

During the years of their existence, these rivers have carried much of the products of erosion past the Blue Ridge to the eastern lowlands and on to the floor of the Atlantic Ocean. Despite the protective cover of vegetation on the mountains, all the rivers run thick with mud during periods of heavy rainfall. When the land high up on the slopes was farmed, even the mountain streams ran muddy.

The contour changes caused by the erosion of mountains occur very slowly when measured by human time scales. No doubt the Appalachian Mountains are being worn away. But it is fair to assume that, unless people themselves level the

Blue Ridge, thousands of generations of humans will yet be able to know the pleasure of walking its ancient mountains.

SUGGESTED READING

GATHRIGHT, THOMAS M. II. *Geology of the Shenandoah National Park, Virginia.* Bulletin 86, Virginia Division of Mineral Resources, 1976.

TAKEUCHI, H.; S. UYEDA; AND H. KANAMORI. *Debate About the Earth.* San Francisco: Freeman Cooper & Co., 1970.

The Forest

Perhaps even more obvious than Shenandoah's mountains are its trees. Every undisturbed land area has its dominant vegetative form; and, as Shenandoah flourishes under each successive year of protective management, it reverts increasingly to deciduous forest.

Although most forms of life on earth have the same basic needs, precise requirements vary greatly from species to species. Since these requirements also vary in their availability from place to place, one area may be better suited to certain organisms than to others. Each type of life survives in those areas where its needs are adequately supplied, and thrives in those areas where its needs are abundantly supplied.

Throughout most of the North American Hardwood Shield (an area of the United States stretching roughly from the Atlantic Ocean to the Mississippi River and from the Carolinas to Canada) the requirements of trees such as oaks, hickories, and maples are so generously provided that they are able to thrive as the dominant plant life.

In general, west of the Hardwood Shield soil moisture becomes a limiting factor, and grasses predominate. To the north, lower temperatures cause most of the hardwoods to give way to firs and spruces. To the south, increased temperatures and reduced moisture (because of more porous soils) give various types of pines the advantage. But such generalities—without actually being inaccurate—can be misleading. There are oak trees in Nebraska and Labrador and Florida—and there are firs and spruces and pines and grasses in Shenandoah!

THE FLORA AND FAUNA

In fact, the northern Blue Ridge has about sixteen hundred different species of higher plants. Of these, fewer than a hundred are the deciduous trees that make up what we call the dominant vegetation. The forest is a community of many life

The vast Hardwood Shield that once covered nearly all of northeastern United States is made possible because available water from rain and snow is greater than the tremendous amount given off by leafy trees. The forest of Shenandoah, situated as it is on the high ground of the Blue Ridge, is frequently shrouded in the clouds that bring that moisture. From the inside a cloud cannot be told from fog or mist, but whatever it is, this one is beginning to thin and let the sun reach the ground once again.

forms. Although each community is usually named for its most obvious plant, the Shenandoah forest would be incomplete without its rose azalea, jack-in-the-pulpit, interrupted fern, mountain laurel, lady slipper orchid, and over fifteen hundred other plants. It would also be incomplete without its white-footed mouse, gray fox, striped skunk, deer, bear, raven, titmouse, barred owl, and nearly three hundred other species of birds and mammals.

WILLIAM S. LEA

The fox of the forested mountains is the gray fox. It dens in hollow logs or under boulders, and will climb trees to reach prey or escape enemies. It is nocturnal and secretive, but its barks are sometimes heard during its spring mating period.

ROBERT C. SIMPSON

The preferred habitat of the wood thrush is deciduous woodland. So, not surprisingly, its range almost exactly coincides with the original boundaries of the North American Hardwood Shield.

HUGH CRANDALL

The snail is a gastropod, a relative of the octopus and the squid. It is also a relative of the chambered nautilus. Its shell however, instead of being pearly and lustrous, is plain and rustic, befitting its woodland habitat.

It needs, as well, its thousand or so species of spiders, twenty to thirty thousand species of insects, and more than a few species each of fish, reptiles, amphibians, mollusks, mushrooms, algae, and bacteria—and one species of crayfish. From any point of view and under any magnification, the forest is a vast and complex society—it hardly seems fair to call it a mere community!

Like a human society, the forest is constantly changing. In the recent geologic past, continental glaciers extended far south of their present limit. Although the last glaciers never reached the latitude of Virginia, their existence as far south as what is now New York and northern Pennsylvania modified the Blue Ridge climate so that this region became covered by a boreal forest of spruces, firs, and related plants.

As the glaciers receded, the seeds of these

A beautiful thistle blossom may conceal a deadly menace. The small spider that holds its legs out to the side and can move forward, backward, or sideways with equal ease is a crab spider, and does not use silk to capture its prey. Its bite is poisonous to flies and bees, and it merely waits in ambush.

plants sprouted farther and farther to the north, and the boreal forest "migrated" in the path of the retreating glaciers to its present position in Canada. But a colder climate can be found by going higher up as well as by going farther north; each thousand feet of increased elevation is accompanied by a 3.6° F. decrease in temperature. So portions of the northern forest moved up the slopes, and their remnants still persist as scattered red spruces and balsam firs at higher elevations in the park.

There is another pattern of plant succession—one which operates over a much shorter time scale than the slow recession of glaciers. When a piece of land has been cleared down to the basic soil (as would be the case after farming or a severe fire), it reverts to its former state through several stages. Each stage is characterized by the different plant species which replace those preceding them until the original, stable, self-perpetuating stage is restored.

JEFF GNASS

Among the needle-bearing evergreens that share Shenandoah with the more common deciduous trees are five kinds of pine. The short-leaf pine and the table mountain pine are rarely seen, so any pine tree you might see will probably be one of the other three. The Virginia pine has two needles per bundle; the pitch pine has three; and this eastern white pine has five.

It takes many different plants and animals to make a forest—the trees are just the most obvious. Here, however, they seem to be only an unobtrusive background for a large group of hay-scented ferns (which do smell like new-mown hay).

Everyone knows that a real forest has to have deep, dark, secret places carpeted with moss. Shenandoah qualifies.

WILLIAM A. BAKE

In an area in which water received by precipitation is greater than water lost through evaporation and transpiration, the "climax" stage will most likely be some sort of forest. In Shenandoah, the climax is usually a deciduous forest. That condition is reached in fifty to a hundred years through seven stages:

Stage 1: The bare, moist, rocky soil.

Stage 2: Annual, herbaceous plants—mostly mostly those whose seeds are wind-borne.

Stage 3: Grasses and perennial herbs.

Stage 4: Mixed herbaceous and woody plants —which have begun to crowd out the grasses.

Stage 5: Woody shrubs and the seedlings of sun-loving trees—which may have sprouted during earlier stages, but grew more slowly than the herbs and grasses.

Stage 6: Sun-loving trees—providing the shade necessary for survival of seedlings of shade-tolerant trees, but at the same time making it less likely that their own seedlings will survive.

Stage 7: Tolerant trees—completing the shading out of the sun-loving, pioneer species which "nursed" them.

Distinct seasonal change is an essential requirement of the deciduous forest. Despite the distorting damage of winter ice storms, this white oak tree has survived in Shenandoah for 200 to 300 years precisely because of winters—and the springs and summers and falls that followed them. Its life processes have continued only because they have been prompted by seasonal cues (changing temperature, changing light intensity, changing day length, changing precipitation).

WILLIAM A. BAKE

Thus the self-perpetuating climax is reached. But again we are generalizing; these stages are not really that clear-cut. They fade from one into another with such overlapping that it is not uncommon to find oak saplings (stage 7) and red cedar (stage 6) growing among annual herbs (stage 2) and grasses (stage 3) which have not quite been crowded out. A rock slide or a fallen tree in a mature forest creates a small clearing which can be taken over for a few years by the sun-loving plants of earlier successional stages.

On many south-facing, well-drained slopes, soil moisture is only marginally sufficient for deciduous trees, and their growth is not decisive enough to replace the pines completely. The result is a stable condition midway between stages 6 and 7—a "pine-oak climax." Plants and animals often behave with ignorant disregard for our fine generalizations and beautiful classification systems.

The "typical hardwood forest" is a theoretical concept as hard to find in the natural world as the "average man." But, like the average man, it can be described with fair accuracy. It contains a great mixture of plants whose principal growth is manifested at four more-or-less distinct levels.

The highest level, or "upper story," consists of the crowns of (usually) several types of deciduous hardwood trees. The "understory" is made up

The pink azalea is one of the earliest of the blooming shrubs of Shenandoah, often flowering brilliantly in mid-March.

DAVID MUENCH

HUGH CRANDALL

The mountain laurel is not a laurel, but an evergreen heath. Its wood is so dense that growth rings can be seen only under magnification. It blooms profusely in May and June.

The blue-eyed grass is not a grass, but a handsome little lily that blooms close to the ground in small, clear areas of the not-so-deep woods.

of a variety of smaller trees and shrubs, all tolerant of shade provided by the foliage of taller trees. The "ground floor" contains a few even smaller shrubs and many herbaceous plants. Still lower, within the soil itself, is a multitude of bacteria and fungi, the decomposers which turn the accumulation of dead plant and animal material back into its basic elements and minerals.

The creation of one of the many possible variations of such a forest would require, to start with, three kinds of oak: white, northern red, and chestnut. A pignut hickory or two and a sugar maple would complete the upper story. The understory would contain younger specimens of the

Indian pipe, a flowering plant that lives like a fungus.

JEFF GREENBERG

Unknown caterpillar feeding on a sassafras leaf. Soon it will wrap itself in insulating silk for the winter, to emerge in spring as a moth or butterfly.

JOHN M. COFFMAN

Sphinx moth larva on fall huckleberry leaves. Sphinx moths are some of the fastest fliers of the insect world. Some are called hawk moths because of their speed, and others are called hummingbird moths because they feed on flower nectar while hovering.

GARY MESZAROS

The Virginia spiderwort blooms from May to August. Like many other plants it is a forest dweller that prefers the boundary areas between woodland and open spaces.

taller trees—spindly saplings pushing sparse crowns upward toward the sun. There would also be serviceberry, chokecherry, mountain holly, and witch hazel. Virginia creeper and probably grape vines would span the middle area with ropy trunks hanging from clutching tendrils high in the upper story.

At eye level, azalea, mountain laurel, and perhaps one of the smaller dogwoods—red osier or alternate-leafed (species without the showy, white bracts of the larger flowering dogwood)—would flower. A little lower still would bloom the wild hydrangea, maple-leafed viburnum, and birch-leafed spirea.

Only a few inches above the ground, wintergreen, pipsissewa, and the ghostly Indian pipe would be found. There would be trillium, bloodroot, baneberry, jack-in-the-pulpit, and a yellow lady-slipper orchid or two. Through the deep layer of accumulated leaves, the mycelia of mushrooms would have sent up fruiting bodies—a group of tiny puffballs, some yellow coral mushrooms, a red cup mushroom close against the base of a tree, and a destroying angel, palely glimmering. A rotting log would be festooned with a cascade of the tiny parasols of orange mycena.

Once, every fourth tree in our typical Shenandoah forest would have been an American chestnut. Now all that remains of this noble tree are mounds of moss, rotting wood, and clusters of sprouts from still-living roots. The sprouts may live for years—they may even bloom and bear fruit—but none can survive to become the huge hardwood tower the parent was.

From that giant they have inherited a disastrous vulnerability to the chestnut blight, a fungus bark disease inadvertently imported from Asia in the early 1900s. But the role of those root clones in our forest, though limited, is eloquent; they stand as living memorials to a species now effectively extinct. "Here lies a root of *Castanea dentata*. Rest in peace."

Turkey-tail fungus adorns the trunk of a dead tree.

Morels are delicious woodland mushrooms tha[t] appear in sprin[g] Called "merkles ("miracles?") in the Blue Ridge area.

Caesar's aman[ita] delectable relat[ive] of the deadliest mushroom of al[l]

The curious striated bird's nest fungus may be found growing on decaying wood.

The yellow coral mushroom is tough and bitter—the ashy coral mushroom, white to gray in color, is delicious.

The yellow lady slipper is perhaps the most striking of the many temperate-zone orchids. Its bloom is large and bright and, unlike the pink lady slipper, tends to grow in large clumps and in more open locations. A rarity among orchids, it has a fragrance.

CONNIE TOOPS

The American chestnut, despite the deadly blight, still sometimes lives long enough to bloom and bear fruit. But today's few nuts in their burr-like husks are only tantalizing reminders of yesterday's bounty.

HUGH CRANDALL

The jack-in-the-pulpit grows rapidly from a bulb in early spring and blooms in April or May. Because its bulb was boiled and eaten by Native Americans, it also is known as Indian turnip. Its brilliant fruit is an August treat for squirrels and mice.

Overleaf: Fall color is seen first at the mountaintops and moves downward at about 100 feet a day. Photo by Jeff Gnass.

23

Springtime along Overall Run on the west side of the Ridge in the north section. Shenandoah's streams more often form cascades than waterfalls, although at another place on Overall Run are the highest falls in the park, measured at 93 feet.

Another inadvertent import is also a problem in the Shenandoah forest. The gypsy moth was introduced from Europe into the Boston area in 1869 for an experimental attempt to develop a hybrid silk moth. The experiment failed. Even worse, some moths escaped from the laboratory and established themselves in the local environment. They have gradually expanded their beachhead in the New World and now constitute a threat to the Blue Ridge hardwoods. Although the gypsy moth caterpillars do not kill trees as quickly and decisively as a disease, massive defoliations are unsightly and weaken trees enough to cause them to become susceptible to diseases and fungi which can kill them.

An as yet unsolved problem in park protection, a gypsy moth larva enjoys its favorite meal, a succulent oak leaf.

Variations On The Forest Theme

Meanwhile, among the ridges and hollows of Shenandoah National Park, the variations on the basic forest theme are almost infinite in number. Just as major climatic conditions determine the general form of the vegetation over large areas, so do very local conditions dictate which specific plants will inhabit each small plot of soil. Moss really does grow more profusely on the north sides of trees. Differences in elevation, slope, drainage, and exposure can combine to form hundreds of different habitats, each with its own microclimate, and each a better place for some plants than for others.

The ravines between the lateral ridges are minor watersheds. In each a small stream drains excess water, seeping through the forest litter, to the larger streams of the lowlands. The earth is moist, and the water reduces the spread of the daily and yearly fluctuations in soil temperature. So plants that require more water and more stable

ROBERT C. SIMPSON

A solitary vireo brings food to its young, hidden in their cradle slung from a fork in a witch hazel bush.

ROBERT C. SIMPSON

The black-and-white warbler is common in the woods and clearings of Shenandoah.

temperatures do well in the hollows. If the ravine has steep sides and faces north, it will receive less sunlight and average temperatures will be lower. Thus the north-facing hollows provide a habitat for hemlocks, while the more open, warmer hollows support tulip trees and sassafras.

When conditions are ideal for hemlocks, the community has fewer members, for Shenandoah has relatively few plants and animals which really like the cold and wet. At such times the understory is sparse and the ground cover limited, but Canada mayflower, wood sorrel, and perhaps a red spruce or yellow birch are present. Veeries and Blackburnian warblers flit through the canopy high overhead, and the red-backed vole scurries through the thick layer of hemlock needles.

In the sun-warmed hollows, conditions are suitable for a much greater variety of life. Tulip trees may dominate the upper story, but they share it with oaks, ashes, maples, and other trees. The understory is rich with flowering dogwood, ironwood, juneberry, redbud, and witch hazel. Rue anemone, toothwort, violets, and wild ginger carpet the ground between clumps of meadow rue and wild hydrangea.

In the spring a lucky forager can find the pitted heads of morel mushrooms poking through the leaf litter under the tulip trees. Deer have watered at the stream and browsed the shrubbery in passing. A black bear has wandered through, turning rocks and rotten logs in search of grubs and ant nests. A bobcat dens in a rocky slope. Striped skunks have left small depressions in the ground where they have dug for insect larvae and large depressions where they have dug for deer mice. Scattered leaves under a chestnut oak reveal the recent passing of a flock of wild turkeys, and record their pause to scratch for acorns and insects. The dainty nest of a red-eyed vireo hangs from the fork of a chokecherry branch.

The boreal redback vole demonstrates the effect of mountains on the distribution of plants and animals. Its range is really across the boreal woods of Canada, but the Appalachians have led it south to Shenandoah.

JOHN M. COFFMAN

The ring-neck snake is small and sleek and completely harmless—unless you're a salamander.

The pileated is the largest of the woodpeckers (as big as a crow), and the only one with a crest. It drills oval nesting holes.

Northern red salamander, like frogs and toads, is an amphibian. It starts life in the water and returns to it to breed.

In the distance the slow, staccato hammering of a pileated woodpecker is followed by the single screaming hoot of a barred owl disturbed in his daytime sleep. A ring-neck snake slides from under a rock to under a log in search of his favorite food, the red-backed salamander. The spiral web of a garden spider spans an open space; the tiny hole in a patch of bare ground is the entrance to a yellow-jacket nest. A chipmunk pauses on a rock and a red-tailed hawk pauses on a branch.

Regardless of the direction the hollow faces, its dominant element is the stream. The excess

The crayfish. This tiny "lobster" of Shenandoah's streams is fiercely predacious on aquatic insects.

The crayfish, in turn, is a favorite prey of the raccoon. Usually nocturnal, the raccoon is sometimes seen ranging a streambed in daylight, turning rocks in search of food.

Big Meadows has been mostly clear of trees since before European explorers reached the Blue Ridge. It is presumed that Native Americans continued to burn an area that was originally razed by a lightning fire. Early settlers grazed their cattle here and probably had vegetable gardens. Because of its historical interest, the National Park Service attempts to preserve it as an open area by a combination of mowing and controlled burning.

precipitation forms tiny seepage areas high up under the crest of the ridge. The seepages coalesce into a trickle, which drops lower and lower and collects more and more drainage from the flanking slopes. Over the ages the stream creates the hollow by cutting deeper and deeper into underlying strata.

Pools form on ledges of harder rock and empty in waterfalls onto other ledges below. In the pools are schools of tiny, black-nosed dace and sometimes brook trout. Crayfish and aquatic salamanders live under the rocks. In the spring the pools are homes for the larval stages of mayflies and caddis flies. The hard heads and huge mandibles of the latter project from the tubes of cemented twigs which protect their soft bodies. A raccoon catches a crayfish and, before eating it, reflexively washes it in the stream from which it came. A water thrush watches from a nearby branch. Water striders drift a few inches downstream and hurry back to drift again.

THE FOREST'S HABITATS

One of the more varied and unusual habitats in the park is Big Meadows, a five-square-mile plateau at an elevation of 3,500 feet on the usually narrow crest of the Blue Ridge. At least part of it has been cleared since very ancient times. Judging from the many stone arrowheads and spear points that have been found there, it was frequently used as a campground and hunting area by the Indians. They may have created the clearing, or they may have taken advantage of an existing opening, the result of a lightning-caused fire. Early settlers expanded the clearing because the level terrain was easy to timber, and it also made good summer pasture for their cattle.

By the beginning of the twentieth century, Big Meadows was a complex of pastures, meadows, and garden plots that stretched from Dark Hollow to Milam Gap and from Black Rock to the drop-off into the Mill Prong watershed. Since the creation of the park, small sections have been kept

ED COOPER

ROBERT C. SIMPSON

Hog Camp Branch in spring. This small stream drains both of the Big Meadows' marshy areas as well as the steep sides of Dark Hollow. There is also a spring near the top to add even more water. As a consequence, it grows quickly from a mere seepage. Only .6 of a mile down the mountain it produces the 70-foot waterfall that is the most visited in the park.

The song sparrow is a common summer resident of the park.

partially clear for buildings, roads, campgrounds, and maintenance facilities. Additionally, about 300 acres east of the Skyline Drive, opposite the Byrd Visitor Center, have been kept clear for historic interest. The rest is reverting to forest.

The underlying greenstone of Big Meadows is impervious to water, and two shallow basins are marshy throughout most of the year. They are classed as intermittent swamps because both basins leak a little, and during long dry periods most of the water runs out. One of the basins is the Big Meadows Swamp, which year by year is gradually disappearing. That is partly because, no longer hindered by browsing domestic cattle, the forest is encroaching more rapidly. Also, wells drilled in the area to help meet the water requirements of the human community have possibly lowered the underlying water table. The second marshy area is in the center of the cleared section east of the Drive. Excess water from both areas drains into Hog Camp Branch and flows through Dark Hollow and over Dark Hollow Falls to the Rose River.

The two small patches of wetlands, the extensive area in various stages of succession, the open meadow, the "fringes" existing at the edges of roads and around building sites, all combine to provide Big Meadows with the greatest plant variety in Shenandoah. Of the probably 114 different species of trees in the park, 14 are represented only in very limited numbers—as ornamentals persisting at old homesites. Of the remaining 100, over half can be found at Big Meadows. A formal floristic study of the entire community has yet to be made, but such a plant list would surely contain the names of at least 800 species.

An area with many different plants and an abundance of different habitats has a variety of animal life as well. All the usual mammals and birds are at least occasional visitors to Big Meadows. It is the only known place in the park where a jumping mouse or a nesting song sparrow can be found. It is the most likely place to hear the whistle of a bob white, the squeak of a little brown bat, or the twittering of barn swallows. Also, it is a great place to spend a spring evening observing the courtship flights of woodcock.

Nearly every one of the many and varied habitats of Shenandoah will have at least some small claim to uniqueness. The following is a short list of examples:

Big Devils Stairs—a deep gash through the rocks, cluttered with huge boulders and very old trees that have survived because they are too inaccessible to be timbered.

Neighbor Mountain—the southern arm of the Jeremys Run watershed and one of only a few places in the park to have white birch, remnants of the earlier boreal forest.

Nicholson Hollow—site of the historic Nicholson Free State and a fine example of what might be called a "tulip tree sassafras climax."

Old Rag Mountain—a popular day hike to the top of the park's oldest mountain. The ridge trail takes hikers over and under ancient Old Rag granite boulders. It has been reported that when the shelter was being built, a mountain laurel shrub was cleared away and its age later estimated at about 600 years! Mountain laurel grows so slowly, and with such little difference between summer and winter growth, that annual growth rings can be seen only under magnification, so the 600-year estimate is suspect. But, just maybe, somewhere on Old Rag is another mountain laurel that is the oldest living thing in Shenandoah.

The Limberlost—a fine grove of very large, very old hemlock trees.

White Oak Canyon—a lovely stream winding past old hemlocks and white oak trees, with 6 waterfalls—one of them 86 feet high.

Hawksbill—at 4,051 feet, the highest point in the park with remnant red spruce and balsam fir forest.

Ferns and hemlocks form natural companions in the cooler, moister micro-habitats of Shenandoah. Here in the Limberlost is a good place to find both.

The white-tailed deer is more of a browser than a grazer, feeding mostly on twigs and leaves rather than grass. So it's a deer of the forest fringes rather than either the deep woods or the prairie. Although it's called the "Virginia deer," it ranges from the Atlantic to the Pacific and through the lower third of Canada and the northern half of Mexico.

Hoover Camp—the fishing camp at the head of the Rapidan River where President Hoover not only escaped from the oppressive heat of Washington, but also entertained foreign notables, including Prime Minister MacDonald of Great Britain.

Laurel Prong—probably the best example of a hemlock-yellow birch climax; the northernmost example of the rhododendron that is so ubiquitous in the Blue Ridge south of Shenandoah; the only place in the park to find painted trillium.

Patterson Field—once a complex of fields and pastureland like Big Meadows, and now the largest area in the park continuing uninterruptedly through successional stages to a forest climax.

Big Run—the largest watershed, the largest wilderness area, and, in 1986, the site of the largest fire in Shenandoah; probably the best place to find trailing arbutus or a sycamore tree.

THREE WHO CAME BACK

Many large animals of the pre-Columbian Blue Ridge—the elk, the wolf, the woods bison, the cougar—are gone, probably forever. But three large animals that once were native to the area, yet were no longer here when the park was established, have returned.

In the 1930s the Virginia white-tailed deer could hardly be found living naturally in the state of Virginia. Evidence of black bear and wild turkey might occasionally be seen in the Allegheny Mountains west of the Shenandoah Valley, but sightings were rare and there were no sightings east of the Valley.

Then, in 1934, 13 deer were released in Big Run and a few more were stocked in the Massanutten Mountains to the west. The Big Run deer survived, and in 1938 deer from the Massanutten group were seen crossing the Valley into the north section of the park. Today the deer population of the park is approaching the carrying capacity of the habitat.

Because deer are browsers that prefer fringe areas, they may easily be seen during most seasons along the Drive and near other open places. Since they often bed down during the middle of the day, early morning and late evenings are the best times to see them.

The black bear came back all by itself, either down the Ridge from Pennsylvania or across the valleys from the western mountains. In 1937, there were 2 black bears sighted; subsequent population estimates have been 10 in 1944, 30 in 1951, and 300 in 1975. Today it is conceded that the black bear density of Shenandoah is the highest recorded in North America.

Even with the large black bear population, there are relatively few bear-human contact incidents. Except for sows with cubs, black bears are solitary animals of the deep woods that don't much care for people. Also, most people would rather see a large, powerful, not-very-bright, wild animal with sharp teeth and long claws from a distance and from a safe shelter. In addition, park visitors are carefully warned about proper food storage and garbage disposal, and the occasional troublesome bear is trapped and relocated out of the park.

The wild turkey, along with the deer and the bear, is a returned native. Once eliminated from the Blue Ridge by heavy hunting, it is again fairly common in Shenandoah. They can be seen in small flocks in the deep woods.

The wild turkey returned to Shenandoah mostly on its own although a few were stocked in the north district. It, too, has thrived and the park's present population of wild turkeys is estimated at 500 to 800 birds. Turkeys usually congregate in small flocks, but since their principal diet consists of acorns, berries, and seeds—supplemented seasonally by insects and grubs—they forage mostly in the deep woods and are not as easily seen as deer.

All three, the deer, the bear, and the wild turkey, are at or near the carrying capacity of the area. However, because the park is narrow and hunting is permitted on the surrounding lands, it is not believed that any drastic steps toward population reduction will have to be taken.

A black bear cub is a great photographic subject—but its 400-pound mother could be standing right behind you thinking you are a threat. Black bears should be treated with respect and caution—and preferably from a distance.

THE FOREST'S SEASONS

The diversity of scenery and life activities at Shenandoah is increased fourfold by its four distinct seasons. They are almost exactly equal to one another in length, but they overlap, so that each seems about four months long instead of the three that are really assigned to it.

The black and white of winter, snow, bare black tree branches against a gray or very pale blue sky, changes slowly into the pastels of spring, as the new leaves appear in a wave that slides quietly up the mountainsides.

The pastels and frenzied blooming of spring eases gently into the intense green of summer. That in turn gives way to the vibrant colors of the dying leaves in fall, and gradually the trees again become black branches against the gray skies of winter.

Also, in a four-season area with average annual rainfalls and snowfalls of about fifty inches each, it can be expected that the weather would provide additional variety, and it does. Spring rains, summer thunderstorms, fogs, quiet snow-

Mist condenses on a fallen red maple leaf in early autumn.

falls, roaring blizzards—each will, for an hour or a day, add its own characteristics to the many aspects of the world of the Blue Ridge forest. Additionally, one weather phenomenon can be experienced only in the mountains, and two others are much more common at higher elevations.

Perhaps two or three times a year an inversion (cold air in the valleys and a layer of warmer air above it) will result in fog at lower elevations while the mountains are bathed in warm sunlight. The mountains rise like islands from an "ocean" of white fluff.

The redbud, also known as the Judas tree, is common at lower elevations in Shenandoah. Like the locust, it is a member of the highly diversified pea family.

Of course, the reverse situation occurs when the valleys are covered by clouds that are low enough to enshroud the mountaintops. That leaves the valley air clear while the mountains are fogged in. In winter and early spring the clouds can be composed of supercooled water droplets just waiting to be disturbed enough to explode into snowflakes. If the wind is very gentle, the droplets will drift slowly through the forest, crystallizing on any twig or blade of grass they bump into. Later, when the fog drifts away or is burned off by the sun, until the frost melts, the forest really does look like a fairyland, or at least a very large wedding cake.

Another phenomenon, one that can be troublesome, can also occur during an inversion. If rain falls from a level of warm air above a layer of freezing air at the surface, instead of soaking in or running off, it freezes on whatever it touches. Unlike the frost of freezing fog, freezing rain forms clear ice that is dense and heavy.

Because the forest is constantly changing, if you come to Shenandoah in search of some particular thing or impression, you may be disappointed. But, if you come willing to accept whatever the current offering may be, you will rarely go away feeling less than well rewarded.

SUGGESTED READING

BRAUN, E. LUCY. *Deciduous Forests of Eastern North America.* Philadelphia, Pennsylvania: Blakiston Co., 1950.

BROOK, MAURICE G. *The Appalachians.* Boston, Massachusetts: Houghton Mifflin Co., 1965.

GUPTON, OSCAR and FRED SWOPE. *Trees and Shrubs of Virginia.* Charlottesville, Virginia: University Press of Virginia, 1981.

MAZZEO, PETER M. *Ferns and Fern Allies of Shenandoah National Park.* Luray, Virginia: Shenandoah Natural History Association, 1981.

SHELTON, NAPIER. *The Nature of Shenandoah.* U.S. Department of the Interior, National Park Service, Natural History Series, 1975.

HUGH CRANDALL

Fir tree at Big Meadows after a severe ice storm. This tree will survive undamaged; but many oak trees, made even more brittle by the cold, will suffer broken limbs.

Fog "oceans" are a reminder of the real ocean that once covered this area for some 300 million years. They also emphasize the "island" nature of Shenandoah.

The Skyline Drive

An important part of the Shenandoah story is the human construction that allows most park visitors to enjoy the scenery and appreciate the story behind the best-known scenic highway in North America—the Skyline Drive.

During the planning stages for a northern Virginia park, it was obvious that selection of the Blue Ridge site would result in a long, narrow park with a very irregular boundary. So even the earliest plans called for access to be provided by a scenic roadway along the crest of the Ridge. President Hoover, wishing to generate jobs in the economically depressed area, and evidently deciding that the road would be a good idea whether or not the park came about, authorized drought relief funds to be used to build it.

Construction of the Skyline Drive was begun on July 18, 1931, and completed in 1939. Except for the national highways that cross the park, it is the only public roadway in Shenandoah. It was built as close to the crest of the mountains as it was

JEFF GNASS

Fall color attracts many thousands of visitors to the Skyline Drive and its magnificent views of the seasonal change.

feasible, and is consequently winding, with many elevation changes. It travels 105 miles to cover the 75-mile length of the park.

All concessioner facilities: hotels, motels, dining rooms, snack bars, camp stores, and service stations are along the Skyline Drive. All Park Service facilities: visitor centers, ranger stations, picnic areas, campgrounds, wayside exhibits (except for the headquarters complex itself), are also located along the Drive.

Because of the Skyline Drive, Shenandoah, more than most national parks, is rewarding to

The Skyline Drive is 105 miles of scenic splendor. It would not have existed except for the need to enable people to experience the wonders of Shenandoah National Park.

The Skyline Drive allows two million visitors a year to get views like this of Shenandoah Valley farmlands and appreciate why they were once called "the breadbasket of the Confederacy."

motorists. You can have a valuable national park experience in Shenandoah without ever getting out of your car. True, you will miss a lot, but you will see a lot too. After 30, 50, or 100 miles of driving through trees and looking out from overlooks at miles and miles of trees, you can get a pretty good idea of the nature of the Hardwood Forest Shield. The winding ups and downs of the roadway will surely tell you about the shape of the Blue Ridge Mountains.

Shenandoah, because it really is a gentle wilderness, is also a great park for walkers, whether casual strollers or serious backpackers. Most of the trails, whether upward to high places or downward into the hollows and stream courses, start from somewhere along the Drive.

The mission of the National Park Service as declared in the basic enabling legislation of 1916 is "...to conserve the scenery and the natural and historic objects and the wildlife [in the lands under its care] and to provide for the enjoyment of the same in such manner and by such means as will leave them unimpaired for the enjoyment of future generations." Since "conserve" is so rarely compatible with "provide for the enjoyment," most actions of the Park Service have to be compro-

mises. That's certainly true of the Skyline Drive. Carving up the landscape to make a road is hardly conserving; but this particular road contributes so much to the enjoyment of Shenandoah that it must be considered an appropriate compromise.

The Skyline Drive has made one other contribution to the Park Service system. A scenic roadway along the crest of the entire Blue Ridge had been the dream of many people since the early 1900s, but the idea had lacked sufficient force for implementation. Then, President Franklin Roosevelt traveled a completed part of the Skyline Drive to visit the first Civilian Conservation Corps (CCC) camp in Virginia. He was so favorably impressed that he authorized federal assistance in the development and construction of the Blue Ridge Parkway.

The Skyline Drive is a window onto the world of the mountain forest—an *open* window that encourages us to step through and immerse ourselves for a time in the land of our forebears—and in a world before there were people.

SUGGESTED READING

HEATWOLE, HENRY T. *Guide to Shenandoah National Park and the Skyline Drive.* Luray, Virginia: Shenandoah Natural History Association, 1988.

Man at Shenandoah

The human history of northern Virginia, as of elsewhere in the world, is the history of human population expansion, technological advances, and changes in attitudes and values.

Our knowledge of the early inhabitants of this area is like our knowledge of its geology, there are no first-hand accounts available. There are only inferences to be drawn from archaeological findings, and from descriptions of the land itself as it was seen by early European explorers. However, recent archaeological research has been careful and extensive, and the early explorers kept records that are still in existence, so those inferences can be drawn with confidence.

The earliest people known to have been in the area were hunter-gatherers. Some ten thousand years ago they left traces of their presence in the Valley and the Piedmont. A Palmer projectile point dated at about 8000 B.C. was found in the mountains at Browns Gap. Dated evidence found at numerous other sites throughout the mountains indicates that the Blue Ridge has been used by people continuously since that time.

Such use, however, has been predominantly seasonal—none of the many sites of pre-Columbian occupancy that have been studied reveals evidence of year-round habitation. Even seasonal occupancy of the higher lands tapered off after reaching a peak three to four thousand years ago. At that time, people of the area developed agriculture and began to depend less on the natural products of the forest. Despite their building agrarian communities in the lowlands and growing crops of corn, pumpkin, and beans, they remained largely hunters and gatherers.

Much of their foraging still took place in the mountains where they gathered chestnuts, hickory nuts, and other food and medicinal plants more common at higher elevations. Since the Blue Ridge rocks, particularly quartzite, were harder than those of the lowlands, they quarried stone from which to fashion their tools. Although their villages and croplands were along the river bottoms of the Piedmont and the Valley, the mountains contributed greatly to their economy and culture.

They employed fire as a method to drive game within range of their arrows and spears. Their fires created clearings in which grasses grew, attracting grazing animals. The ashes of the fires reduced the acidity of the soil, making it more suitable for berry bushes. They probably burned some areas repeatedly—either to trap, within a circle of flame, game to be shot, or to encourage growth of the berries they gathered for food.

A horse-drawn hayrake shares a Piedmont field with the boulders that make such an old-fashioned farm implement still practical.

People seem especially small as they stand among the several-hundred-year-old giants of the hemlock groves in the Limberlost area of Shenandoah.

A hiker looks out toward the north from Little Hogback Overlook on the Skyline Drive. A few miles out there and 2,000 feet lower is Front Royal and the junction of the North and South forks of the Shenandoah River.

Little is known of the tribal structures of the peoples who lived near the section of the Blue Ridge that is now Shenandoah. The people of the nearby Piedmont from about A.D. 800 on were of two small tribes of Siouan stock, the Monacans and the Manahoacs. The people of the Shenandoah Valley are believed to have been divided into many small tribes of which no record has remained. Both they and the Piedmont tribes are known to have been raided frequently by the larger tribes that lived in the surrounding areas. Eventually all the smaller tribes disappeared and can be assumed to have been either absorbed or annihilated by their neighbors.

The overall effect of these pre-colonial peoples on the land, and on the earth itself, was negligible. They burned, but so did lightning. They maintained clearings, but so did the beaver, elk, and bison. They took their food from the land, as did all living creatures, but they killed off no species. They made small portions of the world unsuitable for some life, but only temporarily, and only to make them more habitable for other life. Their Stone Age tools were limited, and their populations were widely dispersed.

The coming of the Europeans to the New World brought a dramatic change in the intensity of human impact. From the beginning the metal tools of the colonists were far superior and they continued to improve. Although the European population remained modest for several decades after initial settlement, it eventually began both a numerical growth and a geographic expansion that has continued ever since. Inevitably, its effect on the natural world has been considerable.

In the early years of colonization, the newcomers had no contact with the Blue Ridge. The first few generations of settlers of the Virginia Colony were so busy establishing and consolidating their positions on the coastal lands that they had no time and little thought for moving on to lands to the west. It was 62 years after the founding of Jamestown in 1607 that the first European explorer reached the crest of the Blue Ridge, and another 47 years before any attempt was made to investigate and explore the "Great Valley" of the "Euphrates River" that lay beyond the first mountain barrier.

One day in March of 1669, John Lederer started off with three Indian guides, traveling west from Jamestown. Nine days later he stood amid patches of snow on Hightop or Hawksbill (his description fits either) and looked across the Shenandoah Valley toward the receding ranges of the Alleghenies beyond. He made three other trips to the Blue Ridge, but eventually returned to his native Germany without ever having aroused any significant interest in his findings.

Several years later, the royal governor of Virginia, Alexander Spotswood, became interested in expansion of his colony and set about to encourage westward migration. In 1716 he led an expedition of gentlemen (really more of a traveling cocktail party) to view the "Great Valley." He crossed the Ridge, probably at Swift Run Gap (existing descriptions of the journey are somewhat ambiguous and it may have been at Milam Gap) just south of Big Meadows.

Perhaps partly because of that expedition, but also because the increasing colonial population prompted expansion into unclaimed territory, the years 1725-1730 saw the establishment of the first small settlements of colonials in the Shenandoah Valley. Both the first settlers and those of later years came from two distinct areas. Some came across the Blue Ridge from eastern Virginia, and others came down the valley from Pennsylvania. They brought with them domestic animals, crop seeds, firearms, steel tools, and a will to "tame the wilderness."

Those five imports caused a considerable change in the environment. Within a hundred years the cougar, wolf, elk, and bison were gone; deer and black bear were seen only infrequently; and the only Indians were visitors from somewhere else. The forests of the valley, the hollows, and any reasonably flat place in the mountains had been either cleared for crops or drastically thinned for timber. European wildflowers bloomed in the sunlight of the new open spaces.

The settlers of the bottomlands harvested crops. Others, either working for themselves or as employees of mining and timber companies, harvested the natural bounty of the forest. The latter group tended to settle close to the mountains, many on land owned by the companies that employed them. The area thrived as a major contributor to the agrarian economy of the new nation, and both groups shared in its prosperity.

Although the soils of the lowlands were rich and enduring, the soil of the mountains was thin and highly susceptible to erosion, and the settlers of the hollows harvested faster than the forest could regenerate. As year followed year, the prosperity of the Piedmont and the Shenandoah Valley increased, while the prosperity of the Blue Ridge dwindled.

The mountain folk of each generation were forced either to leave their land or to remain where they were in a state of increasing deprivation. To leave meant to seek places in the expanding communities around them, or to move higher up on the slopes where the land was even more fragile. Eventually, those electing to move higher on the mountains could go no farther, and the economic gap between the mountaineers and the more prosperous lowlanders continued to widen.

No doubt the upland population always contained those who preferred the aesthetic wealth of the mountains to the monetary wealth of the

JOHN P. GEORGE

Beyond the delicate shades of springtime leaves and blossoms, the rolling fields of a Shenandoah farm are serenely lovely in the light of a setting sun. Views like this make mountain driving worth the effort.

41

Because there were few skilled artisans among the mountain people, glassware like this would have been treasured possessions. Ceramic jugs and crocks would have been more common.

Some of the mountain people whose land was bought for the park were allowed to live out the remainder of their lives in their homes (maintained in livable condition by the National Park Service). Annie Shenk, shown here on her porch in 1972, was the last such resident.

surrounding farmlands. But it is hard to preserve an appreciation of beauty while engaged in a struggle for physical survival, and the life of the mountain people was reduced to little more than just such a struggle. Over the years they had revived or "reinvented" more and more of the Indian techniques of hunting, gathering, and home-crafts, and they continued a marginal existence by adapting and adjusting.

Meanwhile, other developments were taking place. During the Civil War the Shenandoah Valley had been the "breadbasket of the Confederacy." But, after the war, the trials of Reconstruction, the further opening of agricultural lands to the west, and the further expansion of the railway system to transport the products of those lands combined to reduce the importance of western Virginia's agricultural contribution.

Mining activities—copper on the Blue Ridge, iron and manganese on its western slopes—dwindled under the stress of competition from

Chestnut was the preferred wood for most construction because it was straight grained, readily available, and largely rot resistant. All those qualities made it a natural for split-rail fences.

Whiteoak Run starts as seepage from the spongy soil of the Limberlost. Two miles and about 1,000 feet of elevation down Whiteoak Canyon is the first and highest (86 feet) of 6 waterfalls that can be interesting after a dry summer, or awesome in a wet spring.

more profitable sources. Lumbering was already becoming only marginally profitable when the chestnuts, twenty percent of the remaining trees, were killed off by the chestnut blight between 1910 and 1934. Not only the mountain country, but all of western Virginia was in danger of becoming a backwash of the "tide of empire" that had surged on past.

Fortunately, late nineteenth-century development activities had brought new people into contact with the Valley and its encircling hills. Many visitors appreciated the natural beauty here, which, even through the scars of extensive use, was still clearly visible. Their enthusiasm sparked the development of mountain resorts.

Those resorts had three principal effects on the area. One was prolonging the survival of the mountain people by giving them the opportunity to provide goods, services, and local color. The other two factors were much more significant to the region as it exists today: first, the resorts exposed more people to the natural charm of the area; second, they alerted the local population to the economic potential of tourism. Thus, when the establishment of a national park in the southern Appalachians was suggested early in the twentieth century, both the aesthetic and economic values of locating it in northern Virginia had been demonstrated.

SUGGESTED READING

ALEXANDER, EDWARD P. *The Journal of John Fontaine.* Charlottesville, Virginia: University of Virginia Press, 1972.

DEAN, GLORIA. *The Dean Mountain Story.* Potomac Appalachian Trail Club, 1982.

FLOYD, TOM. *Lost Trails and Forgotten People.* Potomac Appalachian Trail Club, 1981.

LAMBERT, DARWIN. *The Earth-Man Story.* Jerico, New York: Exposition Press, Inc., 1972.

The Fox Hollow trail at Dicky Ridge in the northern section of Shenandoah is a self-guiding trail through the remains of two former homesites. In its 1.3 mile length the elevation change is only 310 feet.

Establishing a Park

In 1924 a committee was formed to select a site for the desired southern park. The committee, no doubt besieged by suggestions and arguments advocating the favorite choices of many people, recommended three possible sites: the Great Smokies, Shenandoah, and Mammoth Cave. All three were approved by Congress in 1926.

The selection of the specific site for the northern Virginia park was the cause of a great deal of partisan lobbying. George Freeman Pollock, the entrepreneur who operated the Skyland resort and controlled 5,000 acres of surrounding mountaintop, was the most effective. Once his interest in the proposed park was aroused, his showmanship and boundless enthusiasm were instrumental in causing this particular section of the Blue Ridge to be chosen.

The next obstacle was money. The western national parks had been established on federal land that had merely to be reserved as parkland instead of being opened to homesteading. But land for Shenandoah was privately owned and thus had to be bought, and there was then no precedent or authority for such an expenditure of federal funds.

The venture seemed to be blocked, but again was saved by enthusiasm. More than 24,000 Virginians pledged a total of $1,300,000 in contributions to demonstrate their interest in the park. The legislature of Virginia added another $1,000,000 of state funds, and arranged for blanket condemnation of the land.

Nine years elapsed, occupied with tracing and clearing of titles; with settlement of lawsuits dealing with boundaries and the right of the Commonwealth of Virginia to condemn land for federal use. At the end of that time all litigations were settled, and the state had clear title to more than 250 square miles of the Blue Ridge Mountains.

Virginia presented the land to the United States and, on December 26, 1935, Secretary of the Interior Harold S. Ickes accepted the gift for the people of the United States, and Shenandoah National Park became a reality! At Big Meadows, on July 3, 1936, President Franklin D. Roosevelt dedicated the park "to this and future generations of Americans for the recreation and for the re-creation that can be found here."

Even before the park was officially established, however, two development projects were begun that *could* use federal funds. One was the building of the Skyline Drive with drought relief funds. The second was the creation of the Civilian Conservation Corps (CCC) in 1933. To provide jobs and speed preparation for the probable park, several camps were established in the area that was to become Shenandoah.

The men of the CCC initially had responsibility for fire fighting, fire and erosion control measures, and landscaping the 100-foot right of way for the Drive and its 66 scenic overlooks. After the park was established, the CCC also constructed campgrounds and picnic areas, developed utility systems, and built trails and trail shelters. The last of the park's 6 CCC camps was closed in 1942.

Of all the actions associated with the creation of this park, the most significant was the almost routine condemnation of the land. Such a legislative step to acquire land for government use for roads, buildings, or military installations was common then and is common today. But, in the case of Shenandoah, perhaps for the first time, a government moved to obtain control of a piece of real estate, not as a site for some construction, but to preserve in its natural state.

HUGH CRANDALL

A fisherman tries his luck in the spring torrent of Big Run.

Among the preserved structures at Camp Hoover is this cabin in which former President Herbert Hoover entertained Great Britain's Prime Minister Ramsay MacDonald in October, 1929.

The concessioner at Skyland today offers an experience reminiscent of George Pollack's Skyland resort of the 1920s.

Shenandoah Today

The park today is 300 square miles of mountain forest of which less than 4 percent is developed. In that developed 4 percent, the park is 105 miles of the Skyline Drive and over 500 miles of foot paths, including 90 miles of the Appalachian Trail. It is campgrounds, lodges, snack bars, visitor centers, picnic grounds, horse stables, and the open part of Big Meadows.

Most of all, the park is the mountains and forests of the undeveloped 185,000 acres of the 96 percent that remains a gentle wilderness. It is the mountain tops, the mountain sides, the stream valleys, the waterfalls, and the wildflowers. It is the animal life and the way each species makes its living by adding its weight at the exact place that it is needed to maintain the exact balance a particular community requires. It is the changes blending one into another during the cycle of Shenandoah's four distinct seasons.

Walkers stopping for a snack on a stony crest is a Shenandoah experience that is ageless. The Native Americans did it, and so will our grandchildren.

Such action manifested a distinct change in the philosophy of land use. The Indians and early settlers of America had lived in close kinship with the land, but even they had felt free to alter the natural world to whatever extent was necessary in order to meet their needs. The more sophisticated societies which followed still clung to the ancient Abrahamic concept of land as clay to be molded according to the strength and desires of its owners. The removal from private ownership, and the setting aside of a part of the northern Blue Ridge to be preserved and protected as a national park expressed, at least in part, a new attitude toward the earth.

That act of condemnation stated the opinion of a large group of people that some land is not raw clay still to be given shape, but is a finished sculpture to be enjoyed and appreciated. It said that, in this section of Virginia, the elements of nature are not just random pigments or musical notes to be manipulated and arranged by people, but constitute an already completed artistic composition—the work of a different artist. It gave real value to the thought that human beings should *live* with the earth rather than *compete* with it—that we are *of* the earth, rather than just *upon* it.

SUGGESTED READING

LAMBERT, DARWIN. *Herbert Hoover's Hideaway.* Luray, Virginia: Shenandoah Natural History Association, Bulletin No. 4, 1971.

POLLOCK, GEORGE F. *Skyland: The Heart of Shenandoah National Park.* Berryville, Virginia: Virginia Book Co., 1960.

REEDER, CAROLYN AND JACK. *Shenandoah Heritage.* Potomac Appalachian Trail Club, 1978.

REEDER, CAROLYN AND JACK. *Shenandoah Vestiges.* Potomac Appalachian Trail Club, 1980.

SHENANDOAH NATIONAL PARK

66

STRASBURG

340

Front Royal (North) Entrance
to Washington D.C. - 72 miles

Front
Royal 55

Front Royal (North)
Entrance Station

NATIONAL FOREST

Shenandoah Valley
Overlook

Dickey Ridge
Visitor Center   5

Signal Knob Overlook
Gooney Run Overlook

Low Gap

Compton Gap
10
Jenkins Gap

entonville

Browntown

Hogwallow Flats
Overlook
15

The Peak

Jordan River

Gravel Springs Gap
Range View Overlook
Hogback Overlook   20
Hogback Mtn.

Mathews Arm

Piney River

Elkwallow
25
Pignut Mtn.

Piney River

ny's Run Overlook

Beahms Gap

hree Sisters

ss Mountain Overlook   30
Pass Mtn.

Headquarters
Panorama

Thornton River

Thornton Gap Entrance Station
2304'

Marys Rock

Hazel Mtn. Overlook

Jewell Hollow Overlook   35
Hazel
Mountain

Pinnacles   Pinnacles Overlook

231

y Man Overlook 3100'
Stony Man Mtn.   40
Hughes River Gap
Pinnacle Peak 3401'

Skyland
Thorofare Mtn. Overlook
Highest Point on Drive 3680

ber Hollow Overlook
Whiteoak Falls Trail Parking Area
escent Rock Overlook   45
Old Rag 3268'

sbill Gap Parking Area
Upper Hawksbill Parking area 3630'

Hawksbill 4051'
Franklin Cliffs Overlook
st Peak in Park
50
s Gap Overlook

Dark Hollow Falls
Syria

Meadows
Dark Hollow Falls
Parking

tor Center
nners
Doubletop Mountain
Banco

dge Overlook   Milam Gap
eek Overlook   Camp Hoover
Fork Mountain
55
Hazeltop
oint Overlook   Bootens Gap
ence   Bearfence   Bluff Mountain
Parking 3295' Mountain
n Mountain

Lewis Mountain
Lewis Mountain

s Overlook
60

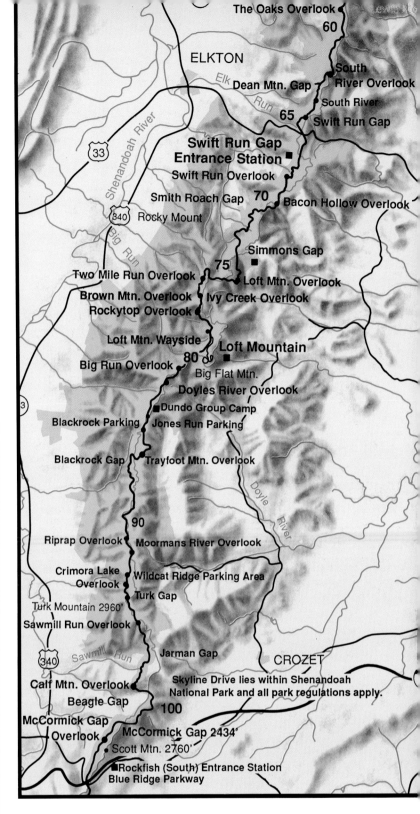

The Oaks Overlook
60

ELKTON
South
River Overlook

Dean Mtn. Gap
South River
65
Swift Run Gap

33

Shenandoah River

Elk Run

**Swift Run Gap
Entrance Station**
Swift Run Overlook

Smith Roach Gap   70
Bacon Hollow Overlook

840   Rocky Mount

Big Run

Simmons Gap
75
Two Mile Run Overlook
Loft Mtn. Overlook

Brown Mtn. Overlook   Ivy Creek Overlook
Rockytop Overlook

Loft Mtn. Wayside   **Loft Mountain**

Big Run Overlook   80
Big Flat Mtn.

3

Doyles River Overlook

Dundo Group Camp

Blackrock Parking   Jones Run Parking

Doyle River

Blackrock Gap   Trayfoot Mtn. Overlook

90

Riprap Overlook   Moormans River Overlook

Crimora Lake
Overlook   Wildcat Ridge Parking Area
Turk Gap

Turk Mountain 2960'

Sawmill Run Overlook

340   Sawmill Run   Jarman Gap   **CROZET**

Calf Mtn. Overlook   Skyline Drive lies within Shenandoah
National Park and all park regulations apply.
Beagle Gap
100
McCormick Gap
Overlook   McCormick Gap 2434'
Scott Mtn. 2760'

Rockfish (South) Entrance Station
Blue Ridge Parkway

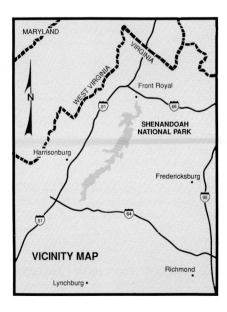

MARYLAND
VIRGINIA

WEST VIRGINIA

Front
Royal

81   66

N

**SHENANDOAH
NATIONAL PARK**

Harrisonburg

Fredericksburg

81   64   95

VICINITY MAP

Lynchburg   Richmond

"The Blue Ridge Mountains of Virginia" has been a evocative phrase for several generations—since long before it was written into the lyrics of a song. It brings to mind visions of gentle grandeur, dignity, beauty, and endurance. In all that time the Blue Ridge has rarely been a disappointment to any who have seen its rocky, tree-shrouded mountains. Nearly two million people come yearly to Shenandoah National Park to test their conceptions against reality.

The reality of Shenandoah today is a 300-square-mile "restoration" project. It can never be made into a "faithful reproduction" of the pre-colonial wilderness of hundreds of years ago. But, by allowing most of the area to recycle itself without interference, it has become a realistic representation of that wilderness.

The restoration is not perfect. Some of the original elements are missing and other exotic elements have been added. There are no woods bison or wolves or passenger pigeons or elk or giant chestnut trees. There are daisies and Deptford pinks and starlings and gypsy moths.

The blue haze of vapor-laden air is often brownish with hydrocarbon pollutants. The rain tests more acid than it would have 300 years ago. But, without the pristine original immediately available for comparison, Shenandoah National Park is a convincing wilderness forest. Among the differences that John Lederer would notice is the most important addition of all—two million dreamers a year—two million people searching for a fragment of reality with which to clothe their dreams so they can dream again with confidence.

Most stories have endings; we prefer the sense of security they provide. But there can be no real ending to any story of the natural world; the forest and the mountains live on. As they live, they change, each change bringing other changes in a widening circle—never ending.

GARY MESZAROS

A doe in the mist at Big Meadows.

Books in the Story Behind the Scenery series: Acadia, Alcatraz Island, Arches, Blue Ridge Parkway, Bryce Canyon, Canyon de Chelly, Canyonlands, Cape Cod, Capitol Reef, Channel Islands, Civil War Parks, Colonial, Crater Lake, Death Valley, Denali, Dinosaur, Everglades, Fort Clatsop, Gettysburg, Glacier, Glen Canyon-Lake Powell, Grand Canyon, Grand Canyon-North Rim, Grand Teton, Great Smoky Mountains, Haleakala, Hawaii Volcanoes, Independence, Lake Mead-Hoover Dam, Lassen Volcanic, Lincoln Parks, Mount Rainier, Mount Rushmore, Mount St. Helens, National Park Service, National Seashores, North Cascades, Olympic, Petrified Forest, Redwood, Rocky Mountain, Scotty's Castle, Sequoia-Kings Canyon, Shenandoah, Statue of Liberty, Theodore Roosevelt, Virgin Islands, Yellowstone, Yosemite, Zion.
NEW: In Pictures — The Continuing Story: Bryce Canyon, Death Valley, Everglades, Grand Canyon, Sequoia-Kings Canyon, Yellowstone, Zion.

Inside back cover: Oak tree silhouetted by the rising sun
Photo by Jeff Gnass

Back cover: Water cascading through boulders in Dark Hollow
Photo by David Muench

Published by KC Publications · Box 14883 · Las Vegas, NV 89114

Printed by Dong-A Printing and Publishing, Seoul, Korea
Color Separations By Kwangyangsa Co., Ltd